Muhammad Ali
The Greatest

Jason Hook

HODDER
Wayland
an imprint of Hodder Children's Books

With thanks to Chris 'The Barber' Erridge, Eastbourne's finest promoter.

© 2000 White-Thomson Publishing Ltd

Produced for Hodder Wayland by
White-Thomson Publishing Ltd
2/3 St Andrew's Place, Lewes, BN7 1UP

Editor: Liz Gogerly
Cover Design: Jan Sterling
Inside Design: Joyce Chester
Picture Research: Shelley Noronha – Glass Onion Pictures
Proofreader: Katie Orchard

Cover: Muhammad Ali training for his World
Championship fight against title holder, George
Foreman, in 1974
Title page: From the cover of Muhammad Ali's LP
'The Greatest' (1963)

Published in Great Britain by Hodder Wayland,
an imprint of Hodder Children's Books

The right of Jason Hook to be identified as the author of
this Work has been asserted by him in accordance with the
Copyright, Designs and Patents Act 1988

A Catalogue record for this book is available from
the British Library.

ISBN 07502 2819 9

Printed and bound in Italy by G. Canale & C.S.p.A.

Hodder Children's Books
A division of Hodder Headline Limited
338 Euston Road, London, NW1 3BH

Picture acknowledgements
The publisher would like to thank the following for their
kind permission to use these pictures:
Action Plus/ Leo Mason 37; Associated Press *(cover)*, 9, 21,
25, 29, 30/31, 40, 43, 45; Christie's Images 6, 33; John
Frost Historical Newspaper Service 39; Hulton Getty
Picture Collection 14, 35; Popperfoto 4, 5, 8, 10, 11, 12,
13, 15, 16, 17, 18, 19, 20, 22, 23, 24, 26, 27, 30 (left),
32, 33, 34, 36, 38, 42, 44; Paul Ray *(title page)*, 10;
Topham Picturepoint 7, 28, 41.

Contents

The Olympic Gold

It is the 1960 Olympic Games. In a boxing ring in Rome, two men battle for the light heavyweight gold medal. A white Polish fighter stands exhausted at the centre of the ring. An eighteen-year-old handsome black American floats around him, shuffling his feet as if he is dancing. The bell rings, and the referee raises the young American's arm and announces him the winner. His name is Cassius Clay.

Cassius Clay fights for gold at the 1960 Olympics.

By the time he won his gold medal, everyone in the Olympic village knew the name of Cassius Clay. He had introduced himself to as many athletes from as many different countries as he could. Some people said it was as if he was running for mayor.

It was clear that the young Olympian had a burning desire to be recognized. But no one suspected that Cassius Clay would become more famous in the next forty years than any sportsman in history. He would be remembered by a different name – Muhammad Ali.

Muhammad Ali, in 1999, receives an award as Sportsman of the Century.

'Clay likes to display supreme confidence by doing intricate dance steps between passages of boxing.'
Sports Illustrated,
29 August 1960.

The Weigh-in

Cassius Marcellus Clay was born on 17 January 1942, in Louisville, the largest city in the American state of Kentucky. He was named after his father, who was a sign painter. His mother, Odessa Clay, cleaned and cooked for wealthy white families. Baby Cassius was nicknamed 'G.G.' after the sound he made when he tried to talk.

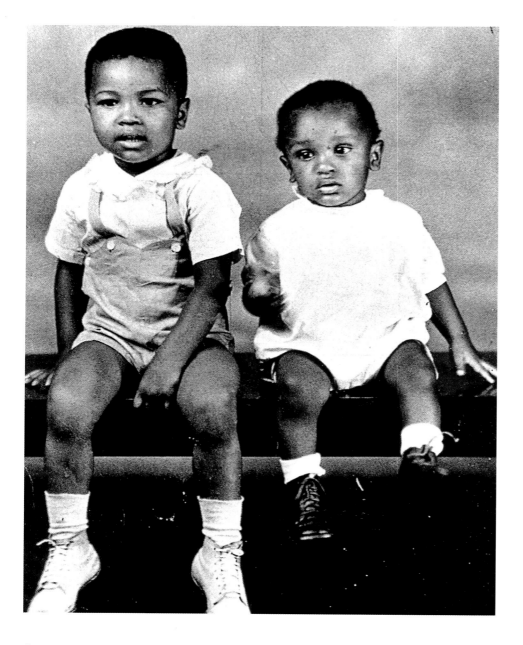

Cassius (left) at the age of four, with his little brother, Rudolph.

'It's like there was a star when he was born that fated him to do what he was going to do and to have impact on mankind around the globe.'
Wilbert McClure, who also won boxing gold at the Rome Olympics.

One of the first black boys allowed into this school in New Orleans in 1960 stands alone in the playground.

Cassius was born into a very different country to today's USA. In states in the South, there were laws that treated black people as less important than whites. They had to travel in the rear of buses, and give up their seats to whites. In Louisville, there were hotels where black people could not stay, shops and restaurants where they would not be served, and schools reserved for white children only.

There were no black baseball players in the Major Leagues until Jackie Robinson made his debut in 1947. Cassius, who was then only five, would grow up to break similar barriers.

The Bell Rings

When he was twelve, Cassius rode to a local fair, ringing the bell on his new red-and-white bicycle. While he was there, the bicycle was stolen. Cassius was led crying to the basement where a policeman named Joe Martin was teaching children to box. Cassius shouted that he was going to 'whup' the thief. In that case, Martin replied, he had better learn to box. From now on, Cassius would hear a different bell ring.

Six weeks later, Cassius Clay made his boxing debut in a three-minute bout. He not only won, but the fight was shown on local television. He now took up boxing with an enthusiasm he never lost. He woke at 5 am every day to go jogging, and at school drew pictures of himself under the title 'World Heavyweight Champ'.

Cassius was tall, quick and totally dedicated. By the age of seventeen, he had won the national Golden Gloves title. He told his mother that he had made his first boxing prediction when he was a baby – 'G.G.' stood for Golden Gloves!

Left *Cassius already shows his boxing style at the age of twelve.*

Right *In training for the Olympics.*

'Boxing made me feel like someone different.' Muhammad Ali recalling his childhood.

Round 1 – The Greatest

After his Golden Gloves success, Cassius flew to the Olympics. He returned to a hero's welcome at Louisville Airport. Cassius then signed a contract with eleven white businessmen to manage him, and began working in Miami with a trainer called Angelo Dundee.

At this time, most boxers let their managers do the talking. But Cassius had seen a wrestler called Gorgeous George attract large crowds by boasting, and now he acted in the same way. He soon became known as the Louisville Lip. Cassius told reporters that he was 'The Greatest!' and 'The Prettiest!'. It did not make him very popular, but more and more people came to his fights – just to see him get beaten!

Float Like A BUTTER FLY Sting Like A BEE

Left *Cassius on the cover of a record of his poems called* I Am The Greatest!

Above *Cassius prepares his stinging punches in training sessions.*

> '*Don't block the aisle and don't block the door.*
> *You will all go home after round four.*'
> Cassius Clay, before knocking out the veteran Archie
> Moore in four rounds.

But in the next three years, nobody could beat him. He made up poems about his opponents, and even predicted the round in which he would knock them out. Cassius was knocked down in his nineteenth fight by Britain's Henry Cooper, but he recovered to win in the fifth round – as he had predicted.

In 1963, Cassius fought Henry Cooper at Wembley, London.

Round 2 – Bear Hunting

The World Heavyweight Champion, Sonny Liston, now agreed to fight Cassius. Liston was a powerful, menacing man, who had spent several years in prison. He had won the title in one round, and some people thought he was invincible.

Cassius clowns with the Beatles, who visited him as he trained for the bout with Liston.

'Though a clown never imitates a wise man, the wise man can imitate the clown.' Nation of Islam preacher, Malcolm X, talking about Cassius Clay.

As he trained for the fight, Cassius was visited by the pop group the Beatles. Many older people in the Sixties felt that things such as Clay's loud talking and the Beatles' loud music were changing the world for the worse. The same people who disliked the Beatles hoped that Liston would shut Clay up once and for all.

Before the fight, Cassius tried everything to upset the champion. He drove a bus to Liston's house painted with the message: 'Liston will go in eight'. He nicknamed Liston 'The Big Ugly Bear', and wore a jacket saying 'Bear Hunting'. When the two boxers were weighed before the fight, Cassius screamed insults at the scowling champion. Liston began to think that maybe his opponent was crazy.

Clay's outrageous behaviour at the weigh-in was part of his plan to upset Liston.

13

Round 3 – Shaking up the World

On 25 February 1964, Cassius Clay fought in Miami for the World Heavyweight Championship. Since the age of twelve, he had boasted that he would win the title. His shorts were white and red, just like his stolen bicycle.

The bell rang, and Liston stalked after Clay. He threw a punch, but Clay had vanished. He threw another. Cassius danced away as quickly as he had at the Olympics. Then Cassius started to land his own stinging jabs. The crowd could not believe it. Cassius was too fast for the ferocious champion.

Cassius battles with the fearsome Sonny Liston.

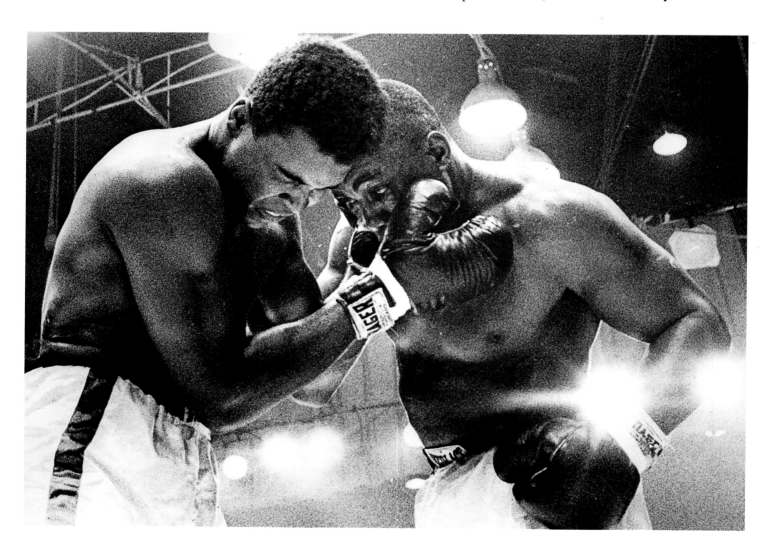

Cassius fought the fifth round almost blind, after a substance smeared on Liston's gloves got in his eyes. But still Liston could not catch him. After the sixth round, a bewildered Liston slumped down on his stool and growled, 'That's it!' It was one of the biggest upsets in boxing history. Cassius Clay rushed across the ring shouting: 'I shook up the world! I shook up the world!'

As Liston quits on his stool, Cassius celebrates his astonishing victory with his cornermen.

Round 4 – Muhammad Ali

After his victory, Cassius gave the USA an even bigger shock. He explained that he belonged to a Muslim group called the Nation of Islam. Their leader, Elijah Muhammad, believed black people should be proud of their race, dress modestly, and avoid drugs and alcohol. The Nation of Islam also preached that black and white people should live separate lives. Many people found this idea very frightening – even though there were hotels at this time where the World Heavyweight Champion could not stay because he was black.

Elijah Muhammad announced that Cassius had been given a new name – Muhammad Ali. He said Cassius Clay was a 'slave name' – a reminder that black people had been used as slaves in the USA and given names by their white owners.

> **'I don't have to be what you want me to be. I'm free to be what I want.'**
> Cassius Clay, at the press conference after the fight.

Muhammad Ali applauds a speech by the Nation of Islam leader, Elijah Muhammad.

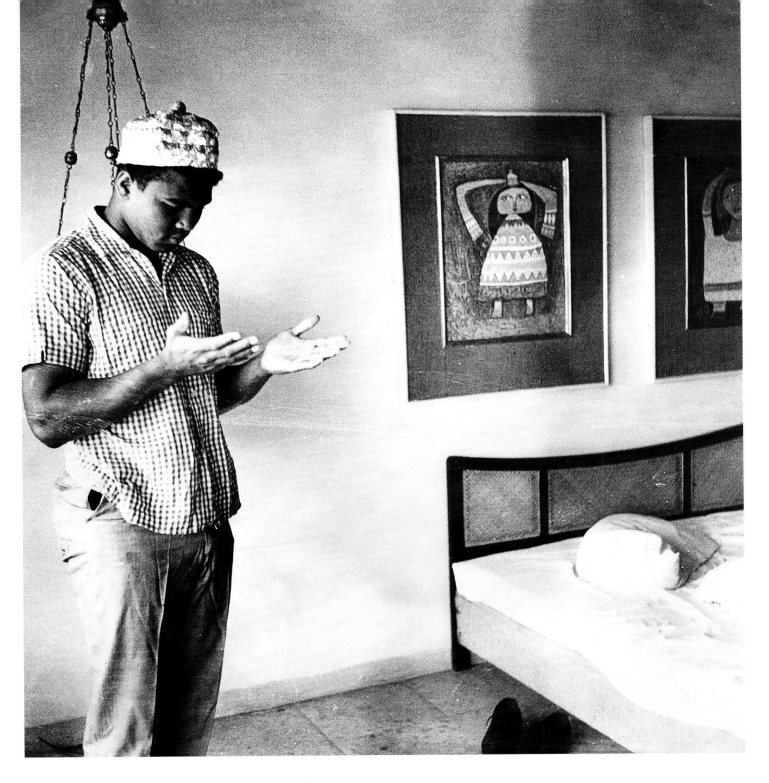

Ali prays during a visit to Africa in 1964.

People now wrote terrible things about Ali, and refused to use his new name. They felt the World Champion should fit in with their ideas of race and religion. But here was a black boxer demanding the freedom to choose not only his own religion, but his own name. Now Ali really had 'shook up the world'.

Round 5 – What's my Name?

In May 1964, the new champion toured Africa. Thousands of Africans, who Ali called 'my true people', turned out to cheer: 'Ali! Ali!' He had suddenly become much more than just a sportsman.

Ali and Malcolm X in 1964, during a visit to Harlem, a poor area of New York.

In 1967, Ali was at the height of his boxing powers. He gave Ernie Terrell a terrible beating after Terrell refused to call him by his new name.

'Muhammad Ali – or Cassius Clay... seems capable of taking care of himself in the exchange of words as well as that of blows.'
Jackie Robinson, the first black baseball player in the Major Leagues, 1967.

In May 1965, Ali knocked Sonny Liston out in the first round with a punch so quick that few people saw it land. Ali later explained that the spectators had all blinked at the same time! In the next two years, Ali gave some of the finest displays in boxing history, defeating eight challengers. One of them, Ernie Terrell, called him Cassius Clay instead of using his new name. So Ali outboxed him for fifteen rounds, all the time asking: 'What's my name?'

Round 6 – Refusing to Fight

US troops at war in Vietnam.

In the 1960s, the USA was fighting a war in Vietnam, south-east Asia, against Communist forces called the Vietcong. Many young men were 'drafted', or forced, to join the army. When he was twenty-two, Ali had taken an intelligence test set by the army, who said his IQ of 78 was too low for him to be drafted. But four years later, even more soldiers were sent to Vietnam. When Ali was told that he might now have to join them, he made a famous remark: 'Man, I ain't got no quarrel with them Vietcong.'

The same newspapers that had attacked Ali for changing his name now called him a traitor. The government also wanted to make an example of him. On 28 April 1967, Ali was forced to line up at a military centre in Houston. An officer bellowed: 'Cassius Clay – Army!' Ali believed the war was against his religion and was prepared to go to jail for his beliefs. He refused to step forward.

Ali is escorted from the military centre in Houston, Texas after refusing to join the US Army.

Round 7 – A Low Blow

Ali talks to the Press outside the court in Houston, June 1967, after receiving his sentence.

When Ali refused to join the army, the boxing authorities stripped him of his title and took away his boxing licence. The government sent him for trial, and the judge gave him the maximum sentence – five years in prison and a $10,000 fine. Ali remained free while his lawyers appealed, but his passport was taken away.

> **'I'm being tested by Allah. I'm giving up my title, my wealth, maybe my future. If I pass this test, I'll come back stronger than ever.'**
> Muhammad Ali, 1967.

Vietnam had become the most important issue in the USA. Ali was banned from boxing for over three years, and during this time people began feeling differently about the war. As television showed young Americans being killed and wounded, protests against Vietnam grew. Ali had made people think about their own beliefs, and to many of them he now became a hero.

During his ban, Ali toured the colleges around the USA. He used the platform that boxing had given him to talk about race, religion and sport. Ali ended his speeches by crying 'Who's the champion of the world?' and his audience screamed back 'You are!'

Students receive Ali warmly during a rally in 1968 at St John's University, New York.

23

Round 8 – Courage

If we had to imagine the greatest heavyweight boxer in history, it would have to be Muhammad Ali fighting between 1967 and 1970 – when he would have been in top condition. But he was not allowed in a boxing ring. He was unbeaten when he was stripped of his title, and looked unstoppable. By the time he returned, he was past his best. But there was greater magic to come, and he would box for ten more years.

Ali's conviction for refusing the draft was overturned in 1971. He had made his boxing comeback the previous year, winning in three rounds. But he had lost his greatest ability, the speed that allowed him to avoid punches. He would replace it with a more dangerous quality – courage.

'The world never saw what might have been. And that's very sad, like knowing a Mozart symphony or a play by Shakespeare was somehow censored out of existence.'
Ferdie Pacheco, Ali's doctor, talking about his ban.

Muhammad Ali prepares for his comeback in 1970.

Ali in 1973, after having his jaw broken by Ken Norton.

In March 1971, Ali lost for the first time when Joe Frazier beat him on points. Ali won his next ten fights, but was beaten again two years later. This time he lost in twelve rounds to Ken Norton, but fought the last ten rounds with a broken jaw. A surgeon said: 'The pain must have been unbearable.'

Round 9 – Smoking Joe

> 'Joe's gonna come out smokin',
> But I ain't gonna be jokin',
> I'll be pickin' and pokin',
> Pouring water on his smokin',
> This might shock and amaze ya,
> But I'm gonna destroy Joe Frazier.'
> Ali before his first fight with Frazier.

Ali had become much more than just a boxer. People with no interest in boxing now watched his fights. Elvis Presley gave him a robe as a gift. People who admired his protest against Vietnam cheered for him. Others hoped to see him beaten. When Ali fought 'Smokin' Joe Frazier on 8 March 1971 – for the title Frazier had won during Ali's ban – an incredible 300 million people watched in forty-six different countries.

Ali and Frazier became bitter rivals. Ali somehow turned their first fight into a struggle between black and white. He said Frazier was the champion of white America. Frazier, who was actually from a poor black family, never forgave him. He became the first boxer to defeat Ali, winning a brutal fight on points after knocking Ali down in the fifteenth round.

Ali enters the ring in a gown given to him by Elvis Presley.

In 1973 and 1974, Ali avenged his only two defeats, beating Ken Norton and Joe Frazier in rematches. But Frazier had already lost the title to George Foreman. Ali would have to beat Foreman to get it back.

Ali, in January 1974, on his way to a unanimous points victory in his second fight with Joe Frazier.

Round 10 – The Rumble in the Jungle

George Foreman was a giant of a man. He had knocked out thirty-seven opponents, and won the title by knocking Joe Frazier down six times. Because of his plodding, pounding style, Ali called him 'The Mummy'. Experts said Ali would need a 'miracle' to beat Foreman.

When he arrived in Zaire to fight Foreman, Ali received a hero's welcome.

> **'Float like a butterfly, sting like a bee!**
> **His hands can't hit what his eyes can't see.**
> **Now you see me, now you don't,**
> **George thinks he will, but I know he won't.'**
> Ali, reciting poetry before the Foreman fight.

Zaire's President Mobutu Sese Seko with Ali and Foreman before the fight.

For the first time in history, the championship was held in Africa, in Kinshasa, Zaire. It was known as the 'Rumble in the Jungle'. Ali was welcomed to Zaire like a long lost son. He had used his fame to encourage black people in the USA to take pride, not shame, in their African heritage. Now he told Africans he was coming home to regain his boxing throne.

Ali spoke with excitement about seeing black people in control of their own country. He jogged on the streets as he had always done. Few people had televisions, but everywhere Ali went they knew his face and cheered him.

Round 11 – The Rope-a-Dope

The fight took place at 4 am, 30 October 1974, in front of 60,000 spectators. In the dressing room, Ali's followers sat with their teeth chattering because they were so afraid for him. He just told them: 'We're gonna dance!'

Ali danced only for one round. He soon realized he was facing a stronger, younger man who he could not outrun. What could he do now? Then Ali found his 'miracle'. He stopped dancing, leant back on the ropes, and let Foreman punch him. People thought Ali had gone mad. But each time Foreman landed his massive blows, Ali whispered: 'Hit me harder!' The more Ali talked, the more wildly Foreman punched. By the eighth round, Foreman was exhausted. Ali stepped forward and knocked him out. He had slain the giant. It was a beautiful act of sporting genius.

An exhausted George Foreman staggers back as Ali lands the punch that won an incredible victory.

While the monsoon rains fell, and people took to the flooded streets to celebrate, Ali could be found sitting quietly with local children, showing them magic tricks.

'Ali was like a sleeping elephant. You can do whatever you want around a sleeping elephant. But when he wakes up, he tramples everything.'
Malik Bowens, African artist and spectator at the Ali-Foreman fight.

As the referee counts Foreman out, Ali raises his arms to celebrate.

Round 12 – The Thriller in Manila

On 1 October 1975, in Manila in the Philippines, Ali stepped into the ring again with his old rival, Joe Frazier. As if the fight would not be hard enough, he made Frazier furious by nicknaming him 'The Gorilla'.

Ali's good looks, his joking and his poems should not hide the fact that he was involved in a brutal sport, and was one of its bravest fighters. His strong faith enabled him to take terrible punishment in the ring and still win. The 'Thriller in Manila' was one of the hardest battles ever seen.

Before their third fight, Ali taunted Frazier by punching a little rubber gorilla!

'It will be a killer, And a chiller, And a thriller, When I get the gorilla, In Manila.'
Muhammad Ali, before his third fight with Joe Frazier.

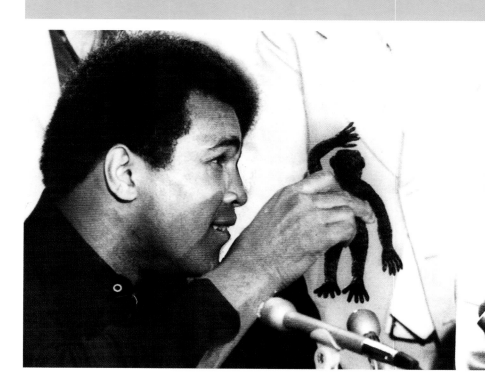

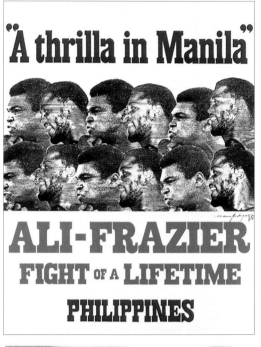

"A thrilla in Manila"

ALI-FRAZIER
FIGHT OF A LIFETIME

PHILIPPINES

Frazier and Ali each landed punches that should have knocked out the other, but both men simply refused to be beaten. Before the final round, Frazier's eyes had become swollen shut. His corner refused to let him carry on. Ali had won, but he slid to the canvas with exhaustion. He said later: 'It was like death. The closest thing to dying I know of.'

Left *A poster advertising the third Ali-Frazier fight.*

Below *Ali throws a punch on his way to an exhausting, hard-fought victory.*

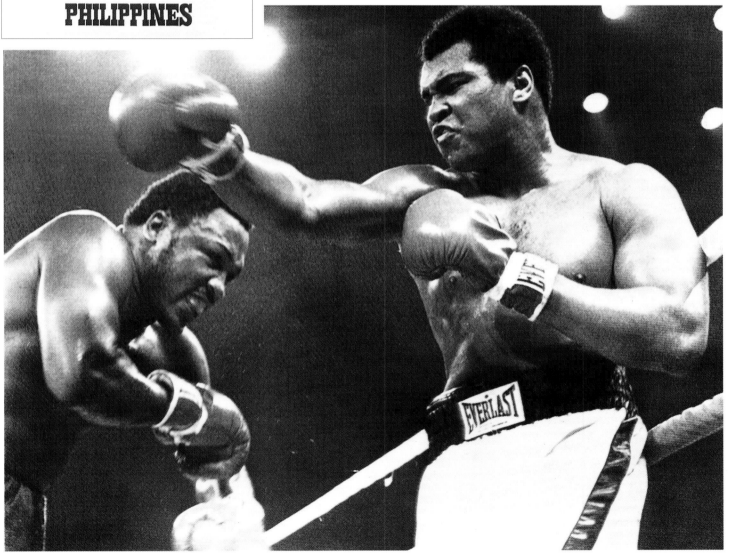

Round 13 – Dancing and Talking

Muhammad Ali was everything a heavyweight boxer was not supposed to be. He was, as he never tired of telling people, pretty. Inside the ring he danced and talked to the crowd. Outside it, he recited poetry and performed an act that people came to enjoy like their favourite soap opera.

Now, every time Ali stepped into the ring, it was not just a fight but a show. On one famous occasion he was even persuaded to fight against a Japanese wrestler – who just lay down in the middle of the ring and kicked his shins!

'It is Ali who has brought to the surface the actor in every athlete.' Bartlett Giamatti, *Harpers Magazine*, 1977.

In 1976, Ali earned over $2 million for fighting Japanese wrestler Antonio Inoki, but the contest was something of an embarrassment.

Right *Ali visits sick children at Great Ormond Street Hospital, London.*

Ali had been an inspiration to many black people around the world. But now he had also become a hero to white people. The way he had fought back to regain his title after being banned and nearly jailed seemed like a fairy-tale. Fans no longer thought about his colour. He was just Muhammad Ali – the most famous face on the planet.

Round 14 – The Final Bell

Ali was getting too old to dance away from punches. He talked about retiring, but he loved boxing too much. People felt that history was being made every time Ali stepped into the ring, so millions of television viewers watched him struggle to six more victories. But each performance was worse than the one before.

On 15 February 1978, Ali fought Leon Spinks, a twenty-four-year-old Olympic gold medallist. It was only Spinks' eighth professional fight. It was Ali's fifty-eighth. Ali was thirty-six and did not train properly, but people were still shocked when Spinks outpointed him.

'To win, all I need to do is suffer.'
Ali, during training for his rematch with Leon Spinks.

Leon Spinks lands a stinging punch during his surprise victory over Ali.

Seven months later, a record crowd watched the rematch.
They wanted to see Ali defeat not just Leon Spinks, but old
age. Round after round, Ali battled to impersonate the quick
feet that had once danced around Sonny Liston, and
rediscover the magic that had trapped George Foreman.
At last, after fifteen long rounds, the final bell sounded.
As the referee raised Ali's arm, the world witnessed the
first man in history to win the heavyweight title three times.

Ali recaptures some of his old magic, on his way to his third world title.

Round 15 – Losing the Fight

Hard blows to the head damage the brain, and Ali had fought over 500 rounds against the hardest punchers in the world. In 1966, he was so fast Cleveland Williams could hit him only three times. But when Ali was older and slower, Leon Spinks landed nearly five hundred punches.

In his later years, Ali no longer had the speed to avoid his opponents' punches. He ended fights battered and exhausted.

In his early days, Clay had been famous for his quick hands and even quicker wit.

'It was like an autopsy on a man who's still alive.'
Sylvester Stallone, after seeing Ali fight Larry Holmes.

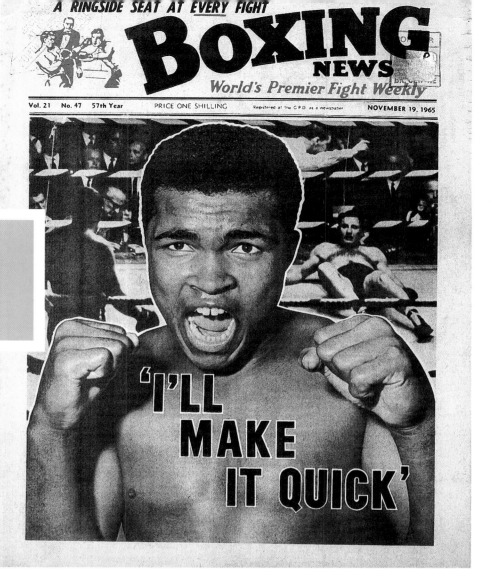

A RINGSIDE SEAT AT EVERY FIGHT

BOXING NEWS

World's Premier Fight Weekly

Vol. 21　No. 47　57th Year　PRICE ONE SHILLING　Registered at the G.P.O. as a newspaper　NOVEMBER 19, 1965

"I'LL MAKE IT QUICK"

Ali had been famous for the speed of his hands and his talking. But in 1980, a medical examination revealed that his speech was slurred. His hands tingled. He even had difficulty touching his nose with his finger.

Ali was sick, and should never have been allowed to box again. But his fame could still earn promoters millions of dollars. At the age of thirty-eight, Ali fought new champion Larry Holmes. A doctor had wrongly prescribed Ali a drug, which left him barely able to lift his arms. For ten terrible rounds, the fastest heavyweight of all time stood still as he was beaten like a rag doll. People prayed for a last glimpse of magic, but there was nothing left.

Retirement

Ali finally retired from boxing at the age of thirty-nine. He had earned more than all the heavyweight champions before him put together, but Ali was famous for his generosity. His millions had been taken by promoters, managers and hangers-on.

In 1984, Ali checked in for tests at a New York hospital.

Ali now had to learn to live without the thrill of his sport. He also faced serious health problems. He was diagnosed as suffering from Parkinson's Syndrome. His condition is similar to Parkinson's Disease, but may have been brought on by the many blows he took during his boxing career.

Today, Ali walks slowly and his hands tremble. Parkinson's Syndrome affects the brain's ability to send messages to the muscles. Ali's face is often frozen like a mask, and he has to make an effort to smile – but when he does he still lights up a room. Most importantly, Ali's intelligence is not affected. His mind is as quick as ever, and his sense of humour has not changed. In 1999, he was still telling journalists that he was planning a comeback!

'Sometimes you won't understand me. But that's okay. I'll say it again.'
Muhammad Ali, 1998.

Ali clowns for the camera after receiving one of his many boxing awards.

Still Magical

Today, Muhammad Ali lives comfortably on a farm in Berrien Springs, Michigan. He is now earning millions of dollars through personal appearances. Ali is loved and looked after by his fourth wife, Lonnie, who grew up near him in Louisville. They have an adopted son, Assad, who is Ali's ninth child. His youngest daughter, Laila, has become a professional boxer.

Laila Ali lands a punch during a professional bout in New York in 1999.

The Center will celebrate the remarkable life and beliefs of Muhammad ... in ... children to pur... dream ... and li...

Ali is winning the hardest battle of his life. He shows no self-pity about his health, and still enjoys watching his old fights. When he shadow-boxes, his trembling hands magically become as quick and steady as they used to be. Ali prays five times a day, and now follows a traditional Muslim belief that supports harmony between black and white people. Ali travels for six months of the year, and still delights in performing magic tricks for children. He can even appear to levitate himself!

By accepting his illness with courage, dignity and faith, Ali has once again become an inspiration to people around the world.

Ali, pictured in his hometown of Louisville in 1998. He celebrates with young fans, the opening of a museum dedicated to his life.

'God's showing me that I'm just a man like everyone else. Showing you, too. You can learn from me that way.' Muhammad Ali in 1998.

The Olympic Torch

It is the 1996 Olympics. In a stadium in Atlanta, Georgia, in America's deep South, a black athlete in a white tracksuit carries the Olympic torch. His hand shakes, but he moves with a magical dignity. Billions of people are watching on television, and every one of them recognizes Muhammad Ali.

Ali's appearance in Atlanta created a wave of emotion. His life had helped to change the lives of many people in the USA. Black athletes could now eat in the same Atlanta restaurants and travel on the same buses as their white colleagues. Ali had made it possible for young sportsmen such as Michael Jordan and Tiger Woods to achieve their goals.

'Muhammad Ali is my hero. He inspired many young black people all over the world to look upon success not as a means of fighting life, but as a means of challenging life's unfairness.' Nelson Mandela, 1993.

Thirty-six years after winning his Olympic gold medal, Ali carries the torch into the Atlanta Olympics.

Today, Ali raises millions of pounds for charity. In 1999, *Time* magazine voted him the most famous man on the planet, and BBC viewers voted him Sports Personality of the Century. He had been Cassius Clay for twenty-two years. He has been Muhammad Ali for thirty-six years. He was, and is, 'The Greatest'.

Ali with athlete Sophia Wesolowsky in 1998, during ceremonies to celebrate the thirtieth anniversary of the Special Olympics.

Glossary

Autopsy A medical examination carried out on a dead body.

Avenged Took revenge for.

Bout Another word for a boxing match.

Censored Removed from public view perhaps because it is immoral.

Communist A system of government used in such countries as the USSR and viewed as a threat by the USA in the 1960s.

Debut The first time somebody appears in public.

Eclipse When a planet blocks the light of the sun, or when somebody outshines or performs better than somebody else.

FBI The Federal Bureau of Investigation, a government security organization in the USA.

Golden Gloves The major amateur boxing championship.

Heritage The culture you inherit from your ancestors.

Invincible Unbeatable.

Light heavyweight A division in which boxers of a certain weight compete.

Monsoon The rainy season in Asia.

Muslim A believer in Islam, one of the world's major religions.

Nation of Islam A religious and political group that supported separating black and white people.

Parkinson's Disease A disease of the nervous system that causes stiffness and tremors in the muscles.

Parkinson's Syndrome The symptoms associated with Parkinson's Disease.

Promoters Business people who arrange events such as boxing matches.

Whup American slang for beat up.

Further Information

Books to Read

For younger readers:

Livewire Real Lives: Muhammad Ali by Julia Holt (Hodder & Stoughton Educational Books, 1998)

For older readers:

Muhammad Ali: The Fight for Respect by Thomas Conklin (Millbrook, 1991)

Muhammad Ali – A Thirty Year Journey by Howard L. Bingham (Robson Books, 1993)

Sources

I'm a Little Special by Gerald Early (ed.) (Yellow Jersey Press, 1999)

King of the World by David Remnick (Picador, 1998)

Muhammad Ali – His Life and Times by Thomas Hauser (Pan, 1991)

Videos

When We Were Kings – The True Story of the Rumble in the Jungle (Polygram, 1996)

Date Chart

1942, 17 January Cassius Clay is born in Louisville, Kentucky, USA.

1959 and 1960 Wins the Golden Gloves Championship in Chicago.

1960, September Wins the gold medal at the Rome Olympics.

1960, 29 October First professional bout against Tunney Hunsaker.

1964, 25 February Wins the World Heavyweight Championship from Sonny Liston.

1964, March Announces he's joined the Nation of Islam and is changing his name to Muhammad Ali.

1964, 4 June Ali marries his first wife Sonji (divorced in 1966).

1965, 25 May Defeats Sonny Liston again, in the first round.

1967, 28 April Banned from boxing for refusing to join the US Army.

1967, 25 June Given a five-year jail sentence for refusing to join the army.

1967, 17 August Ali marries his second wife Belinda (divorced in 1976).

1970, 26 October Makes his comeback against Jerry Quarry.

1971, 8 March Loses for the first time to Joe Frazier.

1974, 28 January Defeats Joe Frazier.

1974, 30 October Defeats George Foreman in the 'Rumble in the Jungle'.

1975, 1 October Defeats Joe Frazier in the 'Thriller in Manila'.

1977, 19 June Marries third wife, Veronica (divorced in 1986).

1978, 15 February Loses his title in the ring for the first time, to Leon Spinks.

1978, 15 September Defeats Spinks, winning the heavyweight title for the third time.

1980, 2 October Beaten by Larry Holmes, attempting a comeback.

1983 Diagnosed as suffering from Parkinson's Syndrome.

1986, 19 November Marries fourth wife, Lonnie.

1990, November Travels to Iraq to help free American hostages.

1993 Meets Nelson Mandela in South Africa.

1996 Ali is given an ovation at the Oscars, where the film of the 'Rumble in the Jungle', *When We Were Kings*, wins an Academy Award.

1996, August Carries the Olympic torch at the opening ceremony of the Atlanta Games.

1999 *Time* magazine votes Ali 'the most famous face on the planet'.
BBC Television viewers vote Ali 'Sports Personality of the Century'.

Professional Record Professional fights: 61 – Won by KO: 37 – Won by Decision: 19 – Lost: 5 (3 of Ali's 5 defeats came in his last 4 fights).

Index

All numbers in **bold** refer to pictures as well as text.